Are You the Christ?

Are You the Christ?

And Other Questions Asked About Jesus

R. Benjamin Garrison

Abingdon   Nashville

Are You the Christ?

And Other Questions Asked About Jesus

Copyright © 1978 by Abingdon

All rights reserved.
No part of this book may be reproduced in any manner whatsoever without written permission of the publisher except brief quotations embodied in critical articles or reviews. For information address Abingdon, Nashville, Tennessee.

Library of Congress Cataloging in Publication Data

GARRISON, R. BENJAMIN.
  Are you the Christ?
  1. Methodist Church—Sermons. 2. Sermons, American. I. Title.
BX8333.G29A73   252'.07   77-11904

ISBN 0-687-01720-3

A portion of chapter 7 is revised from *Portrait of the Church: Warts and All* by R. Benjamin Garrison, Abingdon, 1964. Chapter 6 is based on a homily first published in *Selected Sermons,* an ecumenical sermon-for-each-Sunday service offered by The Seabury Press, 815 Second Avenue, New York, New York 10017.

Scripture quotations unless otherwise noted are from the Revised Standard Version Common Bible, copyright © 1973. Scripture noted NEB is taken from The New English Bible, © the Delegates of the Oxford University Press 1961, 1970. Reprinted by permission. Quotation noted Phillips is taken from the New Testament in Modern English, copyright © J. B. Phillips 1958, 1960, 1972. Scripture noted JB is taken from The Jerusalem Bible, copyright © 1966 by Darton, Longman & Todd, Ltd., and Doubleday & Company, Inc. Used by permission of the publishers. Scripture quotation noted Moffatt is from The Bible: A New Translation by James Moffatt; copyright 1935 by Harper & Row.

MANUFACTURED BY THE PARTHENON PRESS AT
NASHVILLE, TENNESSEE, UNITED STATES OF AMERICA

TO
HELEN ANDERSON MARTIN
mother in love,
beautiful human being,
who was questioning
right up to the day of her death,
in faith.

Preface

Virtually every student of the late Carl Michalson remembers his retelling of an event in the life of the British philosopher R. G. Collingwood. (And, master storyteller that he was, Mike improved the story in the repetition.) Collingwood's little son came to his father one day with the announcement, "I am going to marry Grandma." Perhaps the philosopher was preoccupied that day. Perhaps his intellectual armory contained no weapon with which to fend off that kind of unexpected maneuver. At any rate, the best the father could do was counter, "Well, no; you can't do that. It's not allowed."

"Why not?" replied the boy, irritated. "You married my mother. Why can't I marry your mother?"[1]

Children are not the only persons who can ask unanswerable questions. Cynics can. Saints can. Nearly everybody can.

For a decade and a half or more I have been fascinated by the question category in the ministry of

[1] See Carl Michalson, *The Witness of Radical Faith* (Nashville: Tidings, 1974), p. 69.

Are You the Christ?

Jesus: the questions he answered, the questions he posed, the questions he parried. In an earlier book, *Seven Questions Jesus Asked* (Abingdon, 1975), I offered some of the fruits of that interest.

Are You the Christ? carries that inquiry a step or so further. Herein I am playing the flip side of that earlier record, so to speak—not questions Jesus asked, but questions asked about him. The one exception to this plan is chapter 6, "The Question of Compassion: Who Is My Neighbor?" I maintain, however, that this neighbor question is so central to the message of Jesus that Jesus' answer to it reveals a great deal about his own self-understanding. In fact, whether we are considering the Master Teacher as question or as questioner, the interrogatory category in his thought, when attended to, is an important pointer toward our own self-understanding.

Books are seldom written alone. Mine never are. I am grateful to Dean Larry Andrews of the Graduate College, University of Nebraska, for reading the entire typescript and making numerous helpful suggestions designed to restrain several runaway metaphors and to turn out to pasture some superfluous phrases. I am also pleased to acknowledge the superb work done by Mary Hancock in typing a number of drafts and putting the whole into final form. Other staff members at St. Paul United Methodist Church, Lincoln, assisted by assuming extra duties and thus enabling Mary and me to meet the publisher's deadline.

Sending forth a book, no matter how often one has done so before, involves trepidation combined with excitement and relief. It is a little like sending a child

Preface

off to school. It is too late now for one to help—or to hinder.

In harmony with a recurrent theme in what follows, I do not presume that what I have written will provide many if any final answers to the questions I have chosen. I do hope that it will assist in the formulation of questions that will stretch the reader toward greater faith and faithfulness, deeper understanding, and still further questions.

R. Benjamin Garrison

Contents

I. The Question of Humanity 15
   "What Manner of Man Is This?" 15

II. The Question of Wisdom 26
   "Where Did He Get
      His Wisdom?" 26

III. The Question of Authority 37
   "By What Authority?" 37

IV. The Question About His Meaning 50
   "What Is This That He Says to Us?" 50

V. The Question of Identity 61
   "Are You the Christ?" 61

VI. The Question of Compassion 73
   "Who Is My Neighbor?" 73

VII. The Easter Verb 84
   Index of Scripture 94

Are You the Christ?

1
The Question of Humanity

"What Manner of Man Is This?"
(Matthew 8:23-27)

A few years ago I wrote a book entitled *Seven Questions Jesus Asked*. In the present volume, I propose to look at a different although similar set of problems: not questions Jesus asked, but rather questions asked about Jesus or of him, questions like: Where did he get his wisdom and his authority? What is his message? Is he the Christ? In this chapter the question is, What manner of man is this?

Recently, my family and I changed our residence from Illinois to Nebraska. Consequently and subsequently, I have been doing a good amount of reading in order to acquaint myself with our new cultural home on the Great Plains. In the delightful little book *Shingling the Fog and Other Plains Lies*, Roger Welsch says that in describing the weather in Nebraska "it

Are You the Christ?

hardly seems worth the trouble to lie."[1] He then goes on to point out that Nebraska holds the national record for hailstone size: a pound and a half stone measuring nearly five and one half inches in diameter. He cites official weather sources recording temperatures ranging from −47 to +118 degrees Fahrenheit. Nebraska weather appears to be as temperamental and changeable as people are. For example, the publication the *Nebraska Farmer* relates, with a perfectly straight press, a story about a man who started to chase a deer when he was cultivating corn and had to run him into a snowdrift to catch him!

Well, a storm is the setting for this chapter's Jesus question. The Sea of Galilee, six hundred feet below sea level, is subject to frequent, sudden, and often violent storms. It is, you might say, the Nebraska of the Holy Land. The mountains surrounding the sea are situated in such a way that they function as a series of wind funnels. One day a storm blew up when Jesus and his disciples were out in a boat—most likely a good-sized craft if it contained all twelve disciples plus the Master. Nevertheless, the "boat was being swamped by the waves" (Matt. 8:24). Here the language that is rendered "great storm" means something like "earthquake" or "hurricane"—a great commotion. While the Master's men were scared silly, Jesus himself slept peacefully. They woke him up and appealed for help. The storm then subsided as suddenly as it had arisen. The Jesus question comes next: "What manner of man is this, that even the winds and sea obey him?" (Matt. 8:27 KJV).

[1](Chicago: Swallow Press, 1972), p. 14.

I

Notice first that the disciples asked, "What manner of man is this?" What kind of human being is he?

We need to remind ourselves frequently that Jesus of Nazareth was a man, whatever else we may or may not affirm about him. He did not, like Athena, spring from a god's forehead, full-grown but only half human. When he was cut, he bled; when he toiled, he sweat. The same juices coursed through his body and the same psychic energies pulsed through his being as through our bodies and our beings. He was human—exquisitely human, but human nonetheless.

Yet how often we forget, and forget to teach, that fact. For more than a quarter century I have asked my confirmation classes, young people aged twelve and thirteen, to imagine Jesus as a twelve-year-old. Almost without exception, they find it difficult to picture Jesus heading across the hills with a fishing pole over his shoulder and a dog at his heels. Without some help, they cannot suppose that Jesus ever cried if he was hurt, ever laughed at a good joke, ever played an impish trick on a buddy.

All that these young folks are doing, I submit, is extrapolating from their parents' adult and often dehumanized images of Jesus. In fact, much of our so-called religious art has pictured Jesus as a plastic figure with a weak countenance and a pretty profile—a sort of first-century model for men's shirts. In addition, Jesus comes out looking very un-Semitic—a blue-eyed Anglo-Saxon from Birmingham, England, rather than a dark-eyed, darkskinned progeny of Bethlehem.

Are You the Christ?

The more's the pity, for in so de-manning him, we have cut off our creedal roots. The historic creeds (this is often overlooked) were phrased as much to warn what the early church did not believe as to proclaim what they did believe. They were written to fence out error. Their compilers would never have dreamed of saying that they were fencing in truth in any full or final sense. This observation is of especial relevance to the virgin birth. When the Apostles' Creed came into being (which was, so far as we know, some time in the second century), the idea was abroad that Jesus was not really a man. His temptation in the wilderness was thus no real temptation, for he was God, not man. His sufferings on the cross were a kind of divine playacting—no pain implied, no suffering involved (it just seemed like it)—for he was God.

Actually, the phrases in the creed—"born . . . suffered . . . crucified . . . "—were meant originally to say that Jesus was born as other children were, that he suffered under Pilate as many had, that he was crucified—painfully, inhumanly—like a common criminal. Thus, it is surely an irony that the very phrases placed in the creed in order to strengthen the certainty that Jesus was fully human, instead eventually undermined this certainty.

No. "What manner of *man* is this?" I am glad, and relieved, is a legitimately Christian question and therefore a very human one. Jesus Christ is not an oddity, an exception, not a fine but finally unreachable ideal, as far beyond our stirrings and strivings as is the blazing sun from a burned-out match. If his life were a mere visit, if his humanity were only a charade, then

Christianity would be fiction wrapped in fraud and tied with lies. If Jesus Christ did not share our nature, he could not understand our plight. If he were a divine oddity, then we would be bereft of hope, left to our own destructive devices.

Rather, Jesus is human—*sent to be what we are meant to be.* He is the supreme and supremely compelling example of the power, the potential, and the perfection that belongs to the very process of becoming truly human.

II

So now, more pertinent to our question: What kind of human was Jesus?

First, *Jesus was a confident man.*

Confidence, it is clear, is what Jesus' comrades lacked as they were being battered by the billows on that angry sea. "Save, Lord; we are perishing" (Matt. 8:25). That *sounds* like a pious prayer. They knew they needed saving, and they called upon the Lord. What could be more pious than that? Yet please note that Jesus charged them with unbelief: "O men of little faith" (8:26). That may have been because, as Mark's record makes clear, they mixed their prayer with complaint: "Master, don't you care that we're drowning?" (4:38b, Phillips).

That is, they were engaging more in panic prayer than in pious prayer. Panic prayer is almost inevitable for any of us, human frailty being what it is. Very few of us, I suspect, could honestly claim that we have never prayed a panic prayer, bargained with God, for instance, or tried to. "Lord, get me out of this and I promise that I'll . . . " or "and I promise that I'll never again . . . " But when we thus mis-pray, we are guilty of unbelief, as Jesus said. We signal a lack of the kind of confidence that Jesus so lastingly exemplified.

When we do, it may be caused by what Halford E. Luccock used to call a George B. McClellan complex. General McClellan, you may recall, in the War Between the States failed to deploy his armies victoriously because he was smitten by the delusion that the enemy was stronger than he, even though in fact sometimes (as at Manassas) they were only half as strong as his forces. Mr. Lincoln, saying that McClellan had "the slows," once observed wryly that the enemy must have 1,200,000 troops in the field because every time a Yankee general got whipped he claimed that he was outnumbered three to one.

I think I see about me, and sometimes within me, strong evidence of that debilitating and immobilizing McClellan complex. Because we cannot do everything (any fool knows that), we therefore conclude foolishly that we cannot do anything. Because the hunger or energy crises cannot be easily or cheaply or quickly resolved, we determine by default to do nothing—not to use a calorie or a protein less in our daily diet, not to try a degree lower on our thermostats or a gallon less in our fuel tanks. Because the difficulties in a marriage seem so formidable, we conclude that they are insurmountable and thus let manageable problems bloat into gargantuan ones. Because the challenges to human trust or to religious faith are so relentless, we just quit trying or thinking or praying. A failure of nerve, a

The Question of Humanity

McClellan complex, a collapse of confidence, finds us crying out, like the apostles, "We are perishing."

Hence the perennial appeal of this sublimely confident man named Jesus. He neither underestimated difficulties nor overreacted to them. Toward the close of his ministry, when nearly everything dear to him was coming crashing down around him, he cried out realistically but confidently: "The hour is coming, indeed it has come, when you will be scattered . . . and will leave me alone; yet I am not alone, for the Father is with me" (John 16:32).

III

What manner of man was Jesus? I suggest secondly that Jesus was *a man of calm.*

The gospel writers betoken this lordly calm by contrasting the "great storm" with the "great calm" that followed after Jesus awoke (see Matt. 8:26). (Parenthetically, we see a similar contrast in the next story, in which Jesus heals two emotionally disturbed persons. Their fitful agitation gave way to calming and healing release.) Luke's version of the storm story makes the curious point that the friends of Jesus were afraid not only during the hurricane but afterwards, during the calm. "There was a calm," says Luke, "and they were afraid" (8:24b, 25b).

Afraid during a calm? Yes, some of us would have to admit, if we were honest, that we have been adrift on the waters of calm and that they are sometimes as fearsome as stormy waters. A pastor may wish that a particularly stormy parishioner would shut up and blow away, only to discover that it is far more frightening when there is no longer another person to blame frustrations on. I have counseled with frightfully stormy married couples, only to find that one or both of the partners do not really want a calm solution because then they would have to admit that they are at war within themselves. Mari Sandoz tells us that old "Jules's dugout attracted more and more settlers, for news or to escape the need of living with themselves for an hour or so."[2] Fear of the calm. I suspect further that much of the quiet desperation occurring among the aged is tired testimony to the fact that they miss those trying earlier days when at least they had some storm to battle: kids, job, competitors, the future—something— anything besides this suffocating stillness.

Against all this, and quietly in the midst of all this, stands the calm and calming Son of man. Calm is an elusive quality, difficult to define but, like character, not difficult to recognize. It is an inner atmosphere, a spiritual weather condition that pervades and prevails over both the storms and the silences of life. Because Jesus possessed calm in himself, he was able to offer it to others. "Peace I leave with you; my peace I give to you; not as the world gives do I give to you. Let not your hearts be troubled, neither let them be afraid" (John 14:27). Jesus was a person of pervasive and persuasive calm.

IV

What manner of man is this? I suggest thirdly that *Jesus was a compassionate man.*

---

[2]*Old Jules* (Lincoln: University of Nebraska Press, 1962), p. 81.

The Question of Humanity

I shall spend less time with this quality and characteristic of Jesus, not because it is less important, but because it is more widely recognized and remarked, and because we shall be dealing with it in another chapter. Let us remind ourselves, though, that compassion is an essential characteristic of God. "The Lord was gracious to them and had compassion on them" (II Kings 13:23). Let us remember that Jesus commended it constantly: "But a Samaritan... had compassion... and bound up his wounds," he said, in his most famous and touching parable (Luke 10:33-34). Let us recall that Jesus embodied compassion consistently, bodied it forth, not only toward his own kin and kind, but toward his nation's enemies and his own oppressors also, toward the outcast and the poor. The word *compassion* means literally "suffering *with*," suffering with another or others who need our strength and substance.

If compassion is ever to be seen and shown in the twentieth century, it has to take corporate shape (see below, p. 31). It is relatively easy to be compassionate toward the individual—the one man in the ditch, the single supplicant at the door. Mass society, however, confronts us with the sobering necessity to serve neighbors in the mass. Among the ways to serve plural neighbors are lobbying for better housing, pushing for a cessation of redlining in community loan policies, urging food-stamp practices that serve rather than penalize the poor. It would be easier if neighbor needs came nice and neat and one at a time. But they don't anymore, if indeed they ever did. To be compassionate, then, is to be deliberate about the plural necessities of a complicated and complex world. The politics of compassion may require us to be as deliberate and devoted in confronting the White House or the state-house or the fraternity house as we are in attending the church house.

V

What manner of man is this? I conclude with a fourth mark of the Master. Jesus was not only a confident, calm, and compassionate man, he was also *a calling man.*

Alert readers will have noted that I have moved back and forth in this chapter between these marks of the Master Man and the way those marks are reflected, or ought to be reflected, in us, his people. That, I insist, is altogether appropriate. There is little sense in asking what kind of person Jesus was unless we are willing to make the answer foundational for the kind of persons we are willing to be, by his grace. That is the reason I speak of Jesus as a calling person.

Some readers have seen the contemporary poster bearing the words "God is a verb." That is a profoundly biblical insight. The English tongue is strained to say it so. It would be helpful if we had some word like "God-ing." We come to know what God is by way of what God does: loving, judging, sustaining, encouraging, warning, gracing—Christ-ing. God is a very active verb, reaching into the depths of our struggling, sinning, seeking, hoping, loving, faithing.

We might say, with equal accuracy, that we are to be Christ's active verbs too. His commands are always

The Question of Humanity

distressingly specific: leave your nets, pick up your bed, sell your goods, bear your cross, love your neighbor.

So when I say that Jesus was a calling man, I am saying something about you and me as well as about him.

Maybe this will help you understand. An old story tells of a man who planned to tightrope walk across Niagara Falls, pushing a wheelbarrow before him. When he was about ready to start, a murmur went up through the crowd that it would be suicidal for him to go through with it. In the midst of the warnings, a man came up to the ropewalker and said, "All these people are saying you can't walk that rope to the other side. I believe you can do it, and I want you to know I believe you can." At that the adventurer slapped his encouraging companion on the back and said. "You are the very man I'm looking for. Get into the wheelbarrow. I'll push you across."

Whimsical? Surely. But terribly serious too. If you are really interested in our Jesus question, you will be willing to get into the wheelbarrow—wherever God wants to push you.

II
The Question of Wisdom

"Where Did He Get His Wisdom?"
(Mark 6:1-6*a*)

A hometown boy or girl returns home: entertainer Dick Cavett or Johnny Carson to Nebraska, politician Ronald Reagan to Illinois, astronaut Senator John Glenn to Ohio, author Margaret Truman to Independence, Missouri, musician Marian Anderson to Philadelphia. Sure to emerge on those occasions are the people who "knew them when"—or who imagine they did. "Why, I knew little Ronnie when he was in knee pants" or "little Marian when she sang at the Union Baptist Church."

Those reactions are likely to be a mixture of pride and put-down: "I always knew she was going to be somebody" or "Frankly, he wasn't the best student in the class." Giuseppe Angelo Roncalli, better known

The Question of Wisdom

and beloved as Pope John XXIII, was, like Winston Churchill, a slow starter and a later bloomer. After he had been elected pope, one of his classmates claimed to remember him as the brightest little boy in his class. That judgment, however, probably represents the triumph of piety over accuracy. Bright, Angelo was; studious, he was not, in those early years. His father even predicted that he would be an ineffective priest.

It was much the same when Jesus went back to his boyhood home in Nazareth. His name and fame had been spreading throughout the villages and countryside, bringing attention—sometimes pleasing, sometimes embarrassing—to his native place. When he started his sermon, the sabbath air was electric with eager expectancy. True, some among his hearers, especially the older ones, could hardly see the man for the boy. They were remembering him in whatever was the first-century equivalent of knee pants. They recalled how Joseph let the little tyke "help" in the carpenter shop (parents will understand why that word *help* has to be put in quotes), Jesus being hardly tall enough to see above the workbench or strong enough to lift his end of a plank. Yet despite those memories, or maybe in part because of them, "all spoke well of him" as Luke records this scene in the synagogue (4:22a).

Suddenly, however, the calm became consternation and then clamor, for reasons we shall see later. "All in the synagogue were filled with wrath" (Luke 4:28). As a result, the crowd drove Jesus out of the city and apparently would have thrown him over a nearby cliff had he not escaped. En route they blurted out their question, "Where did this man get all this? What is the

Are You the Christ?

wisdom given to him? . . . Is this not the carpenter, the son of Mary?" (Mark 6:2b-3a). They had known him "when," but had suddenly decided they did not like what they knew—or thought they knew.

I

This event in the synagogue took place during a period in our Lord's ministry that centered chiefly on the area outside of Galilee, which is to say, beyond the jurisdiction of Herod Antipas, Rome's lustful and sadistic local minion. The fact that Jesus' disciples accompanied him on this trip indicates that this was probably not just a personal visit but was incidental to the wider journeys to follow. Anyway, when Jesus' sermon got specific, his hearers got upset.

Both his presence and his presentation had a strong impact. "Many who heard him were astonished," says Mark (6:2). Note that word *astonished*. I do not know quite how to convey the explosion that that word should register. If I could do it audibly, I would shout into a microphone and pound the desk—"Astonished!" In order to communicate it in writing, we would need to italicize it, print it in capitals, underline it, and then add a string of exclamation points—"*ASTONISHED* !!!!!" The crowd of listeners was moved and maddened. But at least they were taking Jesus seriously. I should add that they were taking him wrongly, but at least they were not ignoring him.

I mention this astonishment because it stands in such stark contrast to the way we sometimes treat, and greet, the Master's words. Occasionally, when I am reading scripture in corporate worship, I want to stop and ask the congregation (and myself) "Do you realize what we've just heard? Isn't that astonishing?! It implies revolution—a holy commotion—a veritable storm in the human spirit." The home folks were astonished in a way that stands boldly apart from our sometimes tired, tepid, ho-hum, is-that-so? reaction to the gospel.

The crowd was astonished that Jesus taught— astonished, I mean, that he taught at all. "Isn't he the carpenter?" (One can still hear the sneer—carpenter!) "Why, he's only Mary's son, the very one whose nose we used to wipe." He had attended no theological school, not even a third-rate one. He had studied under no rabbi. He was—well—he was only Jesus. No big deal. A local yokel.

They were engaging in and being trapped by what might be called the fallacy of judging by origins. It is a widespread if pernicious practice, but by no means one that has died out. Paul has an entrancing word to say to his young friend Titus: "Avoid . . . genealogies," he wrote (3:9). In other words, don't get hung up or bogged down by what once was. Don't pay so much attention to your family tree that you have no vital juices left for your own growing.

But so it is, alas! A political proposal is automatically rejected because somebody from the opposition party forwarded it: it is growing on the wrong tree (that is, not on our tree), so we nip it in the bud. It comes from the wrong race or the wrong region or the wrong side of town. So a person or an idea is judged, or esteemed, not on merit but on the basis of what town or century it comes from. Judging by genealogy is, as Halford

Luccock has said, "a powerful and influential way of ... not thinking."[1]

If we were consistent in this near mania about origins (which, fortunately, we are not), we should deprive ourselves of all sorts of cultural riches. The psychologist Gordon Allport has pointed out that, on this dubious basis, we should have to

> disparage the eloquence of Demosthenes because his oratory served as a compensation for his tendency to stammer. We would depreciate Schumann's music because it may have been touched by his psychosis. The rationalism of Kant's philosophy would be invalid because it represented at the outset his protest against the hypochondria induced by his sunken chest. ... Quakerism with its inner voice of guidance would be worthless because the founder of Quakerism, George Fox, suffered severe hallucinations. St. Paul's vision on the road to Damascus would have no significance because it may have been epileptoid in character.[2]

We may surmise that the home folks' rejection of Jesus betokened a deep sense of inferiority: if they could not take him seriously because he had been one of them, then that says something darkly pointed about the low esteem in which they held themselves, out of whose lives he had come.

If, moreover, they were astonished that he taught, they were dumbfounded at *what* he taught. Luke sheds a little light on the content of Jesus' sermon that day in

---

[1] *The Interpreter's Bible* (Nashville: Abingdon-Cokesbury, 1951), 7:727b.

[2] *The Individual and His Religion* (New York: Macmillan, 1950), p. 125.

The Question of Wisdom

Nazareth, which Mark leaves unspecified. Jesus read from the prophet Isaiah. No doubt the gathering nodded approvingly as Jesus intoned these pleasant and venerable lines:

> The Spirit of the Lord is upon me,
> because he has anointed me to preach
>   good news to the poor, . . .
>   release to the captives . . .
>   sight to the blind, . . .
>   liberty to those who are oppressed.
>   (Luke 4:18; cf. Isa. 61:1)

Then he had to go and ruin it all by getting very specific and personal: "Today this scripture has been fulfilled in your hearing" (Luke 4:21). That is to say, "This is what I am about—what *I* am about." So, in the words of a worn but still serviceable phrase, Jesus had stopped preaching and gone to meddling.

It is an old and very sad story. We say we want the way of the Lord to prevail in our lives, in our thoughts, and in our societal structures, but when someone proposes to bring that about in very exacting local and hometown terms, we start looking for some convenient psychological cliff over which to push the culprit. So we are obliged to measure that negative New Testament astonishment against our own. They look very much alike. If Jesus were really to come back today (which is not necessary, for he never really left), can we be so confident that our reaction would be qualitatively different from that of his first-century townspeople? If he were to get meddlingly specific about the poor, the prisoners, and the oppressed here and now, is it not

Are You the Christ?

possible, even likely, that our reaction, too, would be the astonishment of anger?

The astonishment of wonder is, of course, quite another thing. Wonder is something we ought to struggle constantly to protect and express. This is the reason the gospel is often most deeply appreciated by those who are strangers to the faith. Consider a comparison. Novelist Robert Hichens tells of an artist planning to paint a seascape. The artist proposed to portray the power and wonder of the sea as seen and shown through the eyes of a boy. He chose for his model not a lad from Dundee or Dover or Portsmouth, somewhere along the British coast, but a chap from the London slums. Because the boy had never seen an ocean, his eyes and face were flooded with astonishment when first he saw that wondrous water.[3] Beauty—and truth—may be in the eye and heart of the beholder, but some eyes are sharper to see it, and some hearts are readier to burst into astonishment.

That kind of astonishment was not to be on that angry Galilean day. So Jesus had to quote an old proverb. He did so without a trace of cynicism: "A prophet is not without honor, except in his own country" (Mark 6:4a). He was talking about what William Blake calls the film of familiarity. He was talking about the fallacy of the familiar. Can any good thing come out of here?—out of this school or this parish or this town?

Ah, how we cheat ourselves and each other when we so misreason. One of my older friends told me recently,

[3] *Tongues of Conscience* (New York: Frederick A. Stokes Co., 1900), pp. 23-29.

The Question of Wisdom

and with great pride, of a successful physician to whom she had taught chemistry many years ago. The principal in that school, she said, did not think the boy would ever amount to much. Her attitude is reminiscent of Martin Luther's schoolmaster, who habitually removed his biretta when he met his class of boys because—who knew?—among them might be a future mayor or chancellor or doctor!

Another astounding thing about that hometown astonishment is that apparently Mary and the siblings also wondered where Jesus got his wisdom. There isn't the slightest smidgen of evidence that they understood, let alone supported, Jesus in what he had to say. On the contrary, he included them in his laconic lament: "A prophet is not without honor, except in his own country, and among his own kin, *and in his own house*" (Mark 6:4, author's italics).

Here we have the film of familiarity again. It is difficult, close to impossible, really, for some parents to credit the likelihood that one of their children might understand something better than they, the parents, do. Likewise, some young people will listen to advice nearly identical to what they have received at home precisely because it does not come from home. Paul Tillich puts the same truth more positively when, in one of his many excellent sermons, he observes that, on the other hand,

> wisdom is present in parents who know the limits of their authority and do not become idols first and crushed idols later. Wisdom is present in children who know the limits of their independence and do not despise the

heritage they have received and from which they live even in their rebellion against their parents.

II

What is this wisdom that they saw in Jesus? Recall what was said earlier in this chapter about the fallacy of judging by origins. Jesus, in his wisdom, was not guilty of that. On the other hand, he was not careless or ignorant of origins. For example, it has frequently been pointed out that many, indeed most, of his teachings were not original with him. William Cannon has observed that even Jesus' concept of the Kingdom (or the reign of God) is not completely original. Cannon then goes on to argue, persuasively, that the fact that Jesus' teachings are derived does not invalidate them. Jesus' originality lay in the singular use he made of this common heritage (that, and the fact that he *embodied* them, as we shall see). Cannon suggests a parallel:

> The plot of *Hamlet* was not original with Shakespeare. Indeed, the English poet borrowed it from an old play entitled *The Spanish Tragedy*. Yet even a foreign student who is just beginning to master the power and spirit of the English language is able to discern the difference between *Hamlet* and the parent play whence it sprang. Shakespeare borrowed the plot, but then he transformed it according to his own genius, which endowed it with endurance and made it immortal.
>
> Likewise, Jesus in his teaching about the Kingdom of God accepts the plot of Judaism, but what he does with that plot in his own handiwork, and the lessons he draws

The Question of Wisdom

and the truth he declares are those which have been of lasting value to all mankind. . . .

All Jesus' moral precepts, even the Golden Rule, can be traced to their rabbinic source. His worth as a teacher does not lie in what he discovered but in the use he made of the discoveries of others. He acted as if all he taught was true. He was the answer to his own prayer. He spoke with authority, for every day he lived the message he proclaimed.[4]

The wisdom of Jesus is truly original, in one sense, as lived out. We may say of Jesus, as has been said of Shakespeare, "He was more original than his originals."

Biblically speaking, though, that is not enough. Biblically speaking, the wise person is the one who shares in the discernment of moral obligations. According to the Bible, the wise person is he or she who has received wisdom from on high, from God. The Epistle of James puts it this way: "Wisdom . . . is first pure, then peaceable, gentle, open to reason, full of mercy and good fruits, without . . . insincerity" (3:17).

The problem that these Galileans faced (or refused to face) was that they could not distinguish between faith and facts. They had the facts. They really did. But beneath these facts, they failed to discern *the* Fact, namely, Jesus.

The Germans have a fascinating compound for the word *fact*. They speak of the Tat-Wort, the "deed-word." What this points to is the undeniable certainty and reality that fact is fact and truth is true only insofar as both are *done*.

[4]*The Redeemer: The Work and Person of Jesus Christ* (Nashville: Abingdon-Cokesbury, 1951). pp. 105-6.

Are You the Christ?

This, and this alone, is what makes the life and ministry of Jesus authentic. He did what he said, and he said what he did. Tat-Wort—deed-word—means, as my favorite saint, Francis of Assisi, put it, that "a man has only so much knowledge as he puts to work."

What this finally indicates is that Jesus of Nazareth—Jesus of the ageless ages—possessed, preserved, and presented a profound respect for persons. The evidence for this we see throughout the Gospels: the man in the ditch, the woman at the well, the foreigner, the boy in the far fields, the sinner, the Caesar on the throne. Solomon, as he asked for wisdom, made his prayer in these unneglectable words: "Give me now wisdom and knowledge, that I may lead this people; for who is fit to govern this great people of thine?" (II Chron. 1:10 NEB).

We have arrived home. Wisdom is at once a mystery, a necessity, a gift, and a grace. Jesus got his wisdom from its source in God. He gave his wisdom to its goal in God. He loved and therefore he lived. No one loved more widely, and therefore no one lived more wisely, than he. So Wisdom says in the book of Proverbs:

> For he who finds me finds life
> and obtains favor from the Lord.
> (8:35)

III
The Question of Authority
"By What Authority?"
(Luke 20:1-8)

"But, Dad, do I have to?" With that plaint, the question of authority is raised almost daily. The question of authority has, of course, many forms, among them:

"Let me see your fishing license."
"Do you have a search warrant?"
"Was this an excused absence?"
"Who ordained you?"
"How old are you?"
"What right have you in East Berlin—or in Panama?"

Naturally, then, and inevitably, Jesus would be asked for his credentials. In a way, this question, "By what authority?" underlies all of the Jesus questions we are considering in this book.

> The question about who he was: "What manner of man is this?"
>
> The question about his origin: "Where did he get his wisdom?"
>
> The question about the meaning of his message: "What is this that he says to us?"
>
> The question of his identity: "Are you the Christ?"
>
> The question about compassion: "Who is my neighbor?"

In a word, I say, these are but subordinate clauses to the total question we are addressing in this chapter: "By what authority do you do and say these things?" (Luke 20:2, author's translation).

I

Recall the scene. It was one of those several days during which Jesus was in the temple in Jerusalem. There, in the sacred precincts of his ancestral faith and in the presence of trained rabbinical scholars and of appointed religious leaders, Jesus was audacious enough to be "teaching the people ... and preaching the gospel" (Luke 20:1)—*his* gospel. Moreover, he had been making some equally startling claims. So the temple officers came to him and called upon him to say how he dared make such demands. He had been issuing subpoenas to human souls, so they wanted to see his warrant. "By what authority are you doing and saying these things? Who gave you this authority?"

The Question of Authority

(Luke 20:2). Instead of answering directly, Jesus countered with a question of his own (for reasons we shall see later). The temple bigwigs, to their embarrassment, were unable to answer his query. As experts on religion, they were supposed to be able to answer. In turn, Jesus refused to answer their questions or explain his authority. He simply declined to produce his search warrant—but kept on searching.

II

Let us note that the chief priests' question was a natural one. If they had been asked the same question, "By what authority?" they could and probably would have answered. After all, they were chief priests—not just priests but *chief* priests, high priests. They would have said that the source of their authority was Levi, whose tribe and descendants generations ago had been set aside by the nation for holy duties; that is, they were born priests, not made. Even Jesus recognized that they had some authority: after healing the leper, the Great Physician directed him to show himself to the priests for the customary offerings and ceremonies of purification (Mark 1:44).

These men were absolutely clear about their authority. Others of them were elders, older (and presumably wiser) men who had been designated and ordained by their synagogues in the same way that Moses had chosen the seventy elders in the wilderness (Num. 11:16).

Moreover, aside from the fact that they could and did show their spiritual passports (so why shouldn't

Jesus?), the latter had been making some stupendous claims for God and upon God's creatures: tell Caesar where to go; give your goods to the poor; learn when to keep your mouth shut and when to speak up; pay the price of being a good neighbor—and of calling me Lord. Stupendous claims, those—shocking claims to the priests and elders. So we need to manage a little sympathy for their official consternation. If we understand today that Jesus' authority was one of truth and right (rather than of documents and descent), it was by no means clear to people back then, and it probably would not have been clear to us either, even if we had been standing right there listening at the time.

Moreover, if Mark's chronology is correct (see chap. 2), the events of the day before would have given especial force and ferocity to their demands for documentation. That day Jesus had again been hanging around the temple, just as if *he* were a priest or an elder. Suddenly, and without warning, he blew up. He drove out those who were selling animals for religious sacrifice, angrily denouncing them as a "den of robbers" (Mark 11:17).

If we exercise just a sliver of historical imagination, we can reconstruct the holy hand wringing and finger pointing that would have caused. Suppose, just suppose, something even mildly like that were to occur today at, say, a church bazaar. The intruder speaks—shouts—in an outstate accent and wears backcountry clothes. I rather suppose that the pastors and the church administrative board and probably also the police would hear about it pronto.

It was not, one suspects, the Galilean's religious

The Question of Authority

teachings that upset them. Those were, many of them, quite traditional. What shook these folks to the fringes of their priestly garments was that Jesus was stirring up the people. That was the charge at his trial a few days later. And it was true. What bothered the bureaucracy was not so much that Jesus prayed and preached but that some of those among his hearers might be moved to action.

It is ever thus. Alexander Solzhenitsyn has a damning and almost hideously revealing passage in *The First Circle*. It ought to be read by everybody—not least by that frantic fringe of anti-Communists who think they are so unlike the Communists they claim to see under every bed or to hear in every call for change. Writing of the church in Russia, Solzhenitsyn laments: "No one stops them from ringing their bells; they can bake their Communion bread the way they please; they have their processions with the Cross—but they should not have anything to do with civic affairs."[1] Sound familiar?

Anyway, Jesus refused to answer the chief priests' authoritarian question about authority. He had a couple of good reasons for refusing. One was his suspicion that they were not sincere about it. Their question was a cleverly disguised trap. If he said, "My authority is from God," they could charge him with blasphemy (a capital offense). If he said it did not come from God, they could charge him with impertinence and presumption (not a capital offense but enough at least to shut him up). Under these circumstances, rational

---

[1] *The First Circle*, trans. Thomas P. Whitney (New York: Bantam Books, 1969), p. 145.

Are You the Christ?

discourse was impossible. Any answer would have been unconvincing. So Jesus parried their question and declined to discuss it. Leonardo da Vinci put it well: "Anyone who conducts an argument by appealing to Authority is not using his intelligence; he is just using his memory."

More importantly, Jesus refused to answer because the question of *ultimate* authority is unanswerable. Ultimate authority is ultimate authority. That is about all you can say about it. It can no more be defined than God can. To try to do so is to engage in the logical contradiction of presuming to define the higher by way of the lower (like trying to account for the genius of Shakespeare by parsing his sentences or conjugating his verbs or psychoanalyzing his boyhood). Somerset Maugham says in *A Writer's Notebook,* "I am willing to take life as a game of chess in which the first rules are not open to discussion." Ultimate authority is like that too. That's the way it is—period.

At the very least, we may say that our Lord's authority could not have been justified on the priests' and elders' terms. A comparison may help. If you inquire about my authority as a father, I might attempt to answer your question in either of two ways. I might list for you, one by one, the rules I am able, as a father, to enforce. "You may borrow the car provided that you are home by midnight or that you phone if you are unavoidably delayed." Or, "Phone calls are to be limited to fifteen minutes." These rules would tell you something about my authority—or lack of it. On the other hand, I might bypass the rules and attempt rather to suggest the relationship between myself and my

The Question of Authority

offspring, a relationship of which the rules are but a part. That would be a very different answer, because it suggests a very different (and deeper) authority.

Jesus *could* have answered their question on their terms, but the result would have been some roughly religious equivalent to household rules or legal codes. The kind of authority he sought to indicate, however, is not so easily straitjacketed. You can describe it accurately only if you can tell what makes a parent's broken heart hold more love than before (surely, in any literal sense, a logical contradiction).

Of course, some preliminary authority can be justified. That is the reason parents have, for a season, some responsibility in the lives of their children. That is the reason the Jews were right to appoint elders in their synagogues. That is the reason history is to be studied and tradition searched. That is the reason one's national community is normally to be respected (not worshiped but respected). That is the reason, too, that we must distinguish critically between authority and authorities. The distinction is nicely implied in a story that comes from Africa. An English businessman was visiting a planter friend in Uganda. The planter was an enthusiastic hunter. He arm-twisted his very reluctant visitor into going lion hunting with him.

The first night out, the Englishman was so scared that he scarcely slept. Next morning, in short order, the twosome came upon the fresh tracks of what the veteran hunter avowed had to be a full-grown lion. "Tell you what we had better do," said the Englishman brightly. "You go ahead and see where he went, and I'll go back and see where he came from."

Jesus was surrounded by timid folks like that. They were more interested in the historic hunting grounds than in the present hunt, and they justified themselves with "Abraham said" or "Moses said" or somebody out of the past said. "But *I* say to you," countered Jesus again and again. They were quoting authorities. Jesus was exercising authority. Matthew sums it well. "He taught . . . as one who had authority, and not as their scribes" (7:29).

III

It remains for me to try to state what the authority of Jesus implied and entailed. That is a difficult task, in which failure is virtually certain, but I shall make the attempt. Would it help if we were to contract the word *authority* to *author*? An author is one who has written or produced something, combined elements in a new, never-before, way. That is what God has done in Christ. God has taken the elements of humanity, used and abused and broken in a million creations before; combined them with elements of divinity that humans have often sought but seldom found; and brought them together in the man Christ Jesus in a new never-before way. Whatever authority Jesus possessed came from the Author, that is, from God. This illustration is far from perfect, but it may begin to suggest what Jesus meant and why his hearers did not understand. The elders were talking about the punctuation marks that make a poem readable. Jesus was talking about the poem—and about the poet.

The authority of Jesus was the authority of the familiar. One of my teachers, Carl Michalson, used to

The Question of Authority

say that the Bible has not come alive until it makes you turn in your tracks and exclaim, "Somebody spoke my name—somebody spoke my name." Consider an experience that some of you may have had. The first time I landed in England, I had the overwhelming impression that I had come home, that I had been there before, even though I knew for a fact that this was my first time on those shores. That is something of what I mean by the authority of the familiar. It is a kind of spiritual homecoming. Or, put another way, the words and the way of Jesus are like the birth of a baby: it has happened a multiplied million times before. Yet each time it is brand new, unprecedented, and unrepeatable. The authority of Christ's revelation lies in the way he reminds us—makes us mindful again—of what we knew all along.

Again, the authority of Jesus was *the authority of the reasonable.* "Have you not read?" (Matt. 12:3) he inquired. "What do you think?" (Matt. 18:12, and elsewhere) he asked. "Judge for yourselves" (Luke 12:57) he urged. He invited; he beckoned; he hinted; he reasoned; sometimes he even demanded. But, as Charles Jefferson has illuminated, "he never shoved."[2] What Carl Michalson wrote of Kierkegaard may with even more accuracy be said of Jesus: "His efforts to lead men . . . were delicate thrusts and parries, nudges and insinuations which provoked men to move, *but always with their concurrence.*"[3]

---

[2] *The Best of Charles Jefferson,* ed. Frederick R. Stamm (New York: Thomas Y. Crowell, 1960), p. 75.

[3] *The Witness of Kierkegaard* (New York: Association Press, 1960), p. 118; italics added.

Are You the Christ?

Further, the authority of Jesus was *the authority of love*. Another way of saying this is that Jesus had *the authority of shared hazard*. Jesus asks nothing of us that he is unwilling to undergo himself: "Greater love hath no man than this, that a man lay down his life for his friends" (John 15:14). And he did. "Love your enemies" (Matt. 5:44) And he did. Do not be anxious about tomorrow" (Matt. 6:34). And he wasn't. Richard Baxter, who served as chaplain to the king of England and then was imprisoned for his faith, knew whereof, and of whom, he sang when he wrote of our Lord:

> Christ leads me through no darker rooms
> Than he went through before.

This is the authority of shared hazard.

Once more, *the authority of Jesus was an emptied authority*. Paul expressed it unforgettably: "[Christ Jesus] . . . emptied himself, taking the nature of a servant, being born as a mortal, humbled himself even further and became utterly obedient unto death, the death of a common criminal" (Phil. 2:7-8, tr. mine).

I know no way to state that saving fact simply. Paul certainly did not, apparently could not. So who am I to try? Yet I am obliged to try, even if I succeed only in helping you touch the hem of its meaning.

Christ Jesus emptied himself, poured himself out, dispossessed himself. This self-emptying was a "total surrender of his own gain and glory."[4] It is as though a military general were to choose to live the life of a private soldier, as though a skilled surgeon were to

[4] John A. T. Robinson, *The Human Face of God* (London: SCM Press, 1973), p. 166.

The Question of Authority

start emptying bedpans. To a frantic and fallen world, bent upon self-assertion (and therefore bound for self-destruction), Jesus not only talked about giving up personal prerogatives and becoming a servant, he embodied what he commended. He told us. "He who loses his life ... will find it" (Matt. 10:39)—told us—and then showed us.

In the very last paragraph of Matthew's gospel, he has Jesus declare, "All authority in heaven and on earth has been given to me" (28:18). Note that "given" to me. Jesus did not imagine or manufacture his authority. He simply received it—"all authority in heaven and on earth." Here was no silly separation of the sacred and the secular, of the earthly—or even the earthy—and the heavenly, or of the time-bound and the eternal.

I suspect that Matthew put that statement there, right at the climactic end of his Gospel, because he knew that it was a very strange time for a person to have claimed *any* kind of authority, let alone such a universal kind. If a person could claim authority at a time like that, he must have found its secret. The Redeemer's whole world had come crashing down around his head: friends had feared and fled; enemies had mocked and sneered; officers of both temple and throne had first collided and then colluded and then crucified. Yet out of all that loss and desperation had come the confidence to say, "Nonetheless, dear friends, no matter what this all looks like or feels like, still *all authority is given to me.* Clearly, the man was either possessed of a great madness or of a great faith.[5]

[5] I am aware that this is a post-Resurrection statement. Nevertheless, if the Lucan record of the tradition is accurate—if the disciples'

Are You the Christ?

The verdict of the Christian Era has been that it was, of course, a great faith. Yet that claim in itself is of no particular consequence—or at least of no personal consequence—unless you and I appropriate it particularly and personally. Note well what that means for us, what it requires of us. Even Jesus Christ, our emptied Lord, was granted no demonstrated certainty about those things he taught and lived out and had finally to lay down in death. The authority of his faith lay in the authenticity of his venture.

Since we, his servants, are not above our Master, our faith lies in venture too. Michel Quoist, a French priest, has a prayer in which he asks forgiveness for having acted "as though faith were the result of a demonstration."[6]

No! Not so! This is the truth, both for Jesus and for those who would follow him. Faith lies not in documentation, demonstration, and certitude. It lies in venture, trial, and trust. Only then—and in a lifetime of subsequent and equally venturesome "thens"—will the authority of Jesus Christ be clear and compelling to us. Faith is following.

In Shakespeare's play *King Lear*, the earl of Kent returns to offer himself in service to the king. He wants, he says, "to serve him truly that will put me in trust; to love him that is honest; to converse with him that is wise . . . to fear judgment." When the king asks the earl,

---

despair was dissolved only after Pentecost—then this calm claim to authority would indeed have astounded the followers of Jesus, as I have maintained here.

[6] *I've Met Jesus Christ*, (Garden City, N.Y.: Doubleday & Co., 1973), p. 86.

The Question of Authority

"Dost thou know me, fellow?" the earl replies, "No, sir; but you have that in your countenance which I would fain call master." "What's that?" the king inquires. And Kent responds with one word—"Authority" (act 1, sc. 4).

That, in a profound way, is what we come as Christians to do: to serve him, to love him, to converse with him. It may be a long time before you fully understand all that this means. Perhaps you never will. If, however, you are able to say, as countless others have, "You have that in your face which I would call Master," you are ready for this first step, and able for every step to come.

Debate ceases. Discipleship begins.

IV
The Question About His Meaning

"What Is This That He Says to Us?"

(John 16:16-24)

Alfred North Whitehead has said, "So far as concerns religious problems, simple solutions are bogus solutions." That is probably the reason he advises elsewhere, "Seek simplicity—and mistrust it."

It is at the very least a vigorous *part* of the truth to say that people who want a "simple gospel" will have to look somewhere besides the New Testament to find it. But then, of course, what they find will not be the gospel.

To be sure, many of Jesus' sayings, and some of Paul's and the others', are as lucid as a shaft of sunshine. Equally as often, however, these sayings are not immediately clear. We notice this particularly and repeatedly in the Gospel According to John, my favorite

The Question About His Meaning

Gospel. Therein Jesus says things that even those in his inner circle of friends did not understand. His hearers express surprise and perplexity. Then, before explaining an idea (if indeed he does), Jesus repeats it, usually three times.

Some scholars have suggested that this repetition is simply a rabbinical teaching device, used by Jesus in order to arouse interest. However that may be, if often happens that what Jesus says has the aura of a hint about it, which some get, while others do not, or of a riddle, which some can unscramble but others cannot. The Master's meanings are often mantled in mysteries.

It is no wonder, then, that people sometimes asked, as in the passage that lies at the base of this chapter, "What is this that he says to us? . . . We do not know what he means" (John 16:17, 18).

I

Recall the scene. It is late in the day of Jesus' life. Death lurks just around the corner, only a handful of precious hours away. Jesus says to his friends, "A little while, and you will see me no more; again a little while, and you will see me." (John 16:16). Some of the disciples express puzzlement to one another. Jesus senses that they want to ask him what in heaven's name he means, so he opens the way. He explains by way of analogy—labor and childbirth.

> A woman in childbirth suffers
> because her time has come;
> but when she has given birth to the child she forgets
>   the suffering

> in her joy that a [child] has been born into the world.
> So it is with you: you are sad now,
> but I shall see you again, and your hearts will be full
>   of joy,
> and that joy no one shall take from you.
>
> (John 16:21-22 JB)

Perhaps the disciples did not even understand Jesus' explanation. Nevertheless, he let it stand, concluding with a promise that their joy, like that of a new mother, would be full.

I want first to make a couple of general observations about this chapter's question, "What is this that he says to us?" Then we shall turn to a more specific consideration of what Jesus has said in this particular passage.

II

The first thing to be noted is that we, like the apostles and others, cannot always be sure what it is that Jesus has said to us. The ease with which some people assume that they know, most unmistakably, what Jesus meant by this or that—or what he requires here and now—is a source of frequent amazement to me. My amazement sours into resentment when they claim to know for certain what Jesus has said to *me* or requires of *me*.

Some of the alumni of the General Theological Seminary in New York City recall how Dr. Burton Scott Easton, after lecturing on a particularly difficult subject, would ask, "Have you got that clear?" If

The Question About His Meaning

anyone answered yes, the venerable professor would say, "Then you've got it wrong."[1]

My Christian experience, I have to say, is much more like that. With John, Peter, and the others, I find myself rather frequently asking, "What is this that he has said to me?" Jesus Christ may be the answer—in faith I believe he is the answer—but all too often I do not even understand the question. I hear mystery in the man. The closer I come to him, the more he eludes me. About the time I think I am beginning to understand him, I find new dimensions of depth that I have not even begun to plumb. The more I ponder, the more I wonder. Liken it to a great love. After thirty years together, loving and learning and laughing and crying and fighting, you and your husband or wife know a great deal about each other, a great deal more than you did at the beginning, when the two of you were most unmistakably in love. Moreover, the mystery of love has multiplied. So it is with Jesus, or at least I have found him so.

The second observation is this. Notice the nice symbolism in the fact that Jesus takes the initiative to explain what he is saying even before the question is asked. He knows our needs even before we ask him, knows them better than we do ourselves. He has felt the hungers, hurts, and hopes of the human heart—every human heart—yours and mine. He understands that we are sometimes too timid or too scared or too mixed up to ask. So he says, as John tells us he did in our text, "Is this what you are asking?" (16:19). Oftener than not, it

---

[1] Quoted in Leonard Hodgson, *The Doctrine of the Trinity* (New York: Charles Scribner's Sons, 1944), p. 80.

is. Now we know what we wanted to ask. We know that he knows. So the healing begins. That is what makes his way, the gospel, the Good News.

III

Now let us turn more specifically to the apostles' question, which ought to be our question, What has he said to us?

We know Jesus has said something to us about waiting. "A little while, and you will see me no more; again a little while, and you will see me."

Adults sometimes convince themselves that they are better at waiting than the young are. I am not so sure. The reason I am not so sure is that the young have to do so much waiting, or are expected to: waiting until a course of formal education is completed, waiting until a job is secured, waiting until parents will understand and accept, waiting until Momma is off the phone, waiting for sex, waiting until or until or until. For the young, waiting is a frustrating way of life. For many of us, waiting is hellishly hard. Even a twenty-second silent prayer in church drives us up the pew.

So, I say, I'm not so sure that oldsters do much if any better at waiting than the young. In the immediate context of our scripture, "yet a little while" alludes to the Resurrection; in the wider context, it alludes to that time when God's will reigns "on earth as ... in heaven" (Matt. 6:10c). But, whether immediate or eventual, waiting is just about the last thing we want to do. If "they who wait for the Lord shall renew their strength" (Isa. 40:31a), then they who are too impatient to wait upon the Lord shall waste their strength.

Second, Jesus says something to us about pain. General Giuseppe Garibaldi, nineteenth-century Italian patriot, flung the following challenge to his nation's young: "Come to me; for I have such gifts to offer you—forced marches, nights on the hard ground, wounds perhaps, or, it may be, even death itself for Italy."[2]

An eighth-century Greek hymn, which fortunately is still extant, says much the same thing about Jesus:

> If I find him, if I follow,
> What his guerdon here?
> Many a sorrow, many a labor,
> Many a tear.

That old hymn has survived and thrived, I suggest, because, like every great hymn, it is consistent with the gospel of Jesus. Any contemporary advertisement seeking disciples for the Jesus group, if it were honestly written, would sound more like Garibaldi than Madison Avenue. It would quote Jesus' frank warning: "I send you out as sheep in the midst of wolves" (Matt. 10:16). Luke is even more vivid—"as *lambs* in the midst of wolves" (10:3, author's italics). Not only that, Jesus quickly added, but "you will be hated by all for my name's sake" (Matt. 10:22a). Peter has caught the spirit of his Suffering Servant/Lord when he exhorts his parishioners "to pay the same tax of suffering" (I Peter 5:9 Moffatt). We do not like to pay any tax, let alone the

[2] Quoted in *The Interpreter's Bible* (Nashville: Abingdon-Cokesbury, 1952), 8:735a.

tax of suffering. Some advertisement! Some inducement!

The way Jesus strives to make this idea clearer is, as I said earlier, through the analogy of birthpangs. The metaphor of birthpangs is a familiar one to those who are on friendly terms with their Bible. To cite but one of several scriptural examples, Isaiah, speaking of Israel and the coming reign of God, cries out as if God "herself" were in labor:

> Shall I bring to the birth and not cause
>   to bring forth?
>   says the Lord. . . .
> As one whom his mother comforts,
>   so I will comfort you;
>   you shall be comforted in Jerusalem. . . .
> And it shall be known that the hand of
>   the Lord is with his servants.
>   (66:9a, 13, 14)

When Jesus speaks to us of pain, he is recognizing that any human life—at some time probably every human life—will experience what the book of Exodus calls "a darkness so thick it can be felt" (10:21 JB). Think of that! A darkness that can be *felt*. I have felt that kind of physical darkness a few times in my life—encamped in an army tent or afloat on a Wisconsin lake. If you take that dark tent or that black lake, deepen it and darken it and then apply it to the groping life of the soul, such darkness is frightening indeed. Yet that, says Jesus, is exactly what we must expect and be ready for. An old Jewish proverb declares that "the only whole heart is a broken one." Jesus, undeniably a Jew, would agree. And as William Penn said so plainly and poetically: "No pain, no palm; no thorns, no throne; no gall, no glory; no cross, no crown." What has he said to us? Something about pain.

Jesus has also spoken to us of prayer: "Truly, truly, I say to you, if you ask anything of the Father, he will give it to you in my name.... Ask, and you will receive" (John 16:23-24).

John Wesley has a neatly phased comment on this. He says, "Our Lord gives us here a *carte blanche*." That means a white card, blank except for a signature, conveyed with the agreement that the receiving party or person is free to fill in whatever conditions he or she pleases: "Ask *anything* of the Father."

However, Wesley is not quite accurate in calling our prayer card carte blanche, because the signature affixed to it is at once a freeing and a limiting one: it must be "in my name." That is, it has to be signed by Jesus Christ; but some things cannot be asked or prayed for appropriately in the name of Jesus Christ.

What Jesus has done here really is to give us a new way to pray—praying by checking our petitions over against the mind of the Master. "Let this mind be in you, which was also in Christ Jesus" (Phil. 2:5 KJV) The phrase "through Jesus Christ our Lord," so often and easily added to our prayers, is decidedly not merely a cosmetic addition. It is an essential ingredient of Christian prayer. When we use this phrase sincerely, we are saying that we will write on the card of our prayers only that which can be shown to the Savior without shame. Willie, Thomas Klise's main character in the superb novel *The Last Western*, frequently prays

Are You the Christ?

what he calls the listening prayer.[3] The listening prayer is wordless, speechless, silent, still. In it I listen for what God has to say to me, what Christ-like things God wants from me; it is an inpouring rather than an outpouring, a provocation more than an invocation. It is prayer guided and guarded and gathered up by Jesus Christ our Lord.

How many of your prayers would flunk this simple test: would Jesus sign them? Our prayers are sometimes well worded, even sincere, but they are not prayers that Jesus would sign his name to. Yet if he can, then the promise is plain: "Ask, and you will receive."

Jesus has spoken to us not only of waiting, of pain, and of prayer, but also of joy. To return once more to Wesley: In a letter written from Savannah, Georgia, he stated flatly, "True religion or holiness cannot be without cheerfulness." If he is right (and Jesus' words here would indicate that he is), then sour godliness is actual atheism—"that your joy may be full" (John 16:24). Earlier, Jesus had said much the same: "These things I have spoken to you, that my joy may be in you" (John 15:11; see also John 17:13).

My French New Testament renders the concluding phrase from our text, "that your joy may be full," as "that your joy may be perfect." The word for *perfect* is so vivid in French as to impart fresh meaning: it is *parfait*, recalling a dessert so rich and delicious that only the word *perfect* describes it. Reverently, then, we hear the promise—"that your joy may be like a parfait."

Henceforth, this is to be the mark of the Master's

[3](Niles, Ill.: Argus Communications, 1974), p. 166 *passim*.

The Question About His Meaning

people, and so the mark of us—joy. But note very well, note very soberly, the hard underside of that truth. If joy is to be the mark of the Master's people, then plainly we must be people of joy if we are to be the people of God. The Sad Sacks and Calamity Janes, for all their alleged realism, are not on the side of God because they are not on the side of joy. Isaiah could have written, and it would have been just as true, that "the people who walked in sadness have found a great joy." It is not a Pollyannaish attitude: "Everything's going to turn out all right, and besides I hope I escape the pain." Rather, it is *the joy of finding the rainbow in the only place rainbows can be found—in the rain.* It is knowing what the French poet Paul Louis Claudel meant when he said, after he had heard Beethoven's Fifth Symphony, he knew that at the heart of the universe there is joy. When Haydn was criticized for the "gaiety" of his church music, he replied, "When I think of God my heart is so filled with joy that the notes fly off as from a spindle." That could have been said by Jesus of Nazareth. It *was inspired* by him—"that your joy may be full."

Paul has a wonderful Haydn-like passage at the very heart of his letter to the Romans. It is so full of gladness in God that the church, with wisdom, insight, and art, has planted the words at the very center of the funeral office. Paul has been talking about "the suffering of this present time" (Rom. 8:18). He acknowledges that the whole of creation has been in travail, like a woman in labor. But something is aborning, something marvelous and mysterious. Then he breaks out in a libretto of joy:

Are You the Christ?

> We know that in everything God works for good with those who love him, who are called according to his purpose.... What then shall we say to this? If God is for us, who is against us?... Who shall separate us from the love of Christ? Shall tribulation, or distress, or persecution, or famine, or nakedness, or peril, or sword?... No, in all these things we are more than conquerors through him who loved us. For I am sure that neither death, nor life, nor angels, nor principalities, nor things present, nor things to come, nor powers, nor height, nor depth, nor anything else in all creation, will be able to separate us from the love of God in Christ Jesus our Lord (Rom. 8:28, 31, 35, 37-39)

That is what Jesus has said to us. So thanks be to God, who gives us the victory—and the joy—through Jesus Christ our Lord.

V
The Question of Identity

"Are You the Christ?"
(Luke 22:66-71)

An anonymous poem, rather ordinary except for its title, is addressed to Jesus and proclaims, "Still Thou Art Question."

Indeed Jesus is. As we observed in the previous chapter, about the time we think we are beginning to understand Jesus, new and unplumbed dimensions of depth appear. The New Testament questions that we have been exploring in this book, therefore, and others we could have included, have a place or a counterpart in the twentieth century: What sort of person is this elusive Master? Whence his wisdom and authority? What is his word for us today? What can he show and tell us about compassion?—about the neighbor? What does it mean to be really alive?

Are You the Christ?

The answers I have been struggling to set forth are necessarily fragmented, for we, too, only "know in part" (I Cor. 13:12). Hence that anonymous poem could as well have been entitled "Still Thou Art *Questioner."* One can realistically imagine that Jesus is asking us, as he asked Phillip long ago, "Have I been with you so long, and yet you do not know me?" (John 14:9a). Yea, Lord, you have—but we don't. Like so much of the Bible, that first-century question "Are you the Christ?" remains relevant today.

I

Once again we need to remind ourselves of the question's biblical lineaments. Judas has done his dark thing. "Morning gilds the sky" but slowly—as if the sun itself is reluctant and ashamed to be seen shining on this dreadful day. The elders, up all night, gather in the Hall of Hewn Stones, one of the council chambers or courtrooms of the temple. There they say to Jesus, "If you are the Christ, tell us" (Luke 22:67a). Notice that Luke, unlike Mark (14:61) has cast the elders' puzzlement in the form of a command rather than a question. So Jesus replies, "You wouldn't believe me if I told you" (vs. 67b), adding the terse reminder that they surely would refuse to answer *his* questions. Then he says, almost to himself (as if knowing that it would do no good to speak to them), "But from now on the Son of man shall be seated at the right hand of the power of God" (vs. 69). The reference is apparently to a verse in the book of Daniel (7:13), recalling something Jesus had learned in the synagogue school as a boy. That was

The Question of Identity

enough for the elders. Too much. "What further testimony do we need?" they said. "We have heard it ourselves from his own lips" (vs. 71).

The early church, as we shall see, was quick to claim the title "Christ" for Jesus. The Master himself, however, appears to have been less clear about accepting it. Only once in the New Testament is Jesus remembered as having accepted the title "Christ" for himself in so many words (Mark 14, 61b-62). Matthew and Luke, however, recall it differently, remembering him answering ambiguously, so that his meaning could be taken in more than one way. Most scholars think that the weight of probability is with Matthew and Luke— not "I am the Christ" but something more like "That's what you say." Note that it was frequently the Master's method to answer a question with another question, or to refuse to answer, or to reply in a way that could have more than one meaning ascribed to it. Hence it is likely that Jesus neither clearly affirmed nor categorically denied that he was "the Christ."

The infant church, however, had barely learned to take its first steps before it was proclaiming that the answer was, "Yes, he is the Christ." (And what we have here is the early church speaking.) In fact it was so quick and so clear about it that the title "Christ" (which means "the Anointed" or, in Jewish terms, "Messiah") very soon became not just an appended title but in effect an integral part of Jesus' name. Jesus (who is) the Christ was quickly being called Jesus Christ. We read this in Paul, who uses the terms "Jesus Christ" and "Christ Jesus" quite interchangeably, with no apparent distinction between the two.

On this matter the entire New Testament agrees: Jesus is the Christ, the Anointed One, the Messiah, the Long-Awaited One. Peter's words to Jesus "Thou art the Christ" (Matt. 16:16 KJV)—words Jesus commanded him, for then, to repeat to no one else—are a shorthand summary of the very heart of the primitive Christian faith. Whatever else the New Testament writers disagreed about (and they disagreed about much), however variously they phrased it (and they said it in almost as many different ways as there are books in the New Testament), on this issue they were solidly united. They differed about (and sometimes fought over) the role and realm of the Jewish law, about whether the gospel belonged to those outside Israel, about the virgin birth, about the relationship between faith and works (creeds and deeds), about when and how Jesus would come back to claim his kingdom. Still, differ as they did and as much as they did, on this pivot point they agreed: Jesus, the executed rabbi, is the Christ.

That being so, I propose to alter the question. I do so on quite defensible biblical grounds. The question was not "Are you the Christ?" For the apostles, the answer obviously was yes. Rather, their crucial, more precise, queries were, "Who is this Christ? What does it mean that *Jesus* is the Christ? What does seeing that, saying that, and accepting that require of us?" Moreover, I want to try to answer these Christ questions in what for me are personal terms.

By this I do not mean exclusively personal terms, of course. The Christian faith is not just a personal possession; it is community proclamation. Indeed, if

The Question of Identity

the Bible is any test (and there can be no if about that for Christians), Christian faith is corporate before it is individual. In considering this question, as we consider any other great question about our faith, we are surrounded by "so great a cloud of witnesses" (Heb. 12:1). This plural witness, this corporate testimony, must be listened to before I, as individual, can have any assurance that my own personal witness has any value or verity.

II

Who is Christ for me?[1]

Christ for me is a Jew.

I do not say merely that Christ was in origin a Jew, but that *Christ is essentially a Jew*. I confess, sadly, that Christ's Jewishness is not something I have always apprehended and appreciated.

A story grows out of World War II. The shells were falling fast. In the midst of the battle were ten American boys of Jewish faith. One had been fatally wounded but before he died, he'd asked that the Kaddish, the Jewish prayer for the dead, be intoned over his body. His

---

[1] I am aware that in this section and to some extent throughout this book, I am using the word Jesus and the word *Christ*, alone and in combination, somewhat interchangeably. I appeal, as justification, to the Pauline usage above on page 63, and to the following quote: "These two [terms] are utterly inseparable in the New Testament. They cannot even be thought of apart. There is no word about Christ which is not referred to Him who suffered under Pontius Pilate, and which is not at the same time intended as the Gospel applicable to all persons of every time and in every place" ("The Jesus of History" in G. K. A. Bell and G. A. Deissman, eds., *Mysterium Christi* [London: Longmans, Green & Co., 1930], p. 49).

buddies prepared to carry out his last wish, tenderly lifting his body into the only shelter they could find, the bomb-shattered remnants of a Roman Catholic Church. Then one of the ten remembered that according to Jewish law, the Kaddish could not be said without ten adult Jews present. But there were only nine. In twenty minutes, according to company orders, they were to move out. What to do?

Just then came an ominous silence. Suddenly, the battle broke out again, more furiously than before. As the men flung themselves upon the floor of the church, a mighty explosion caved the rest of the walls in around them. The air cleared. The soldiers prepared to leave.

As they stood there, they stared in amazement. Now they were ten. The figure of Christ had slipped free from the cross in the sanctuary and was standing among them, leaning against a pillar, erect—one of their number. The tenth Jew was in their midst. They said the Kaddish for their buddy and then returned to battle.[2]

That story speaks to me.

Though we may choose to deny it, and tragically often we have denied it, Jesus the Jew is, for Christians, our forefather in the faith. The claims of Jewish religion are "taken seriously—even where critically—on every page [of the Gospels]."

> The petitions of the prayer which He taught his closest followers are with one exception drawn from Jewish

[2] Paraphrased from Maeanna Cheserton-Mangle's "Tenth Jew" in H. E. Luccock and F. I. Brentano, *The Questing Spirit* (New York: Coward-McCann, 1947), p. 250.

sources. When asked what a [person] should do to inherit Eternal Life, He replied in the words of the Torah; and declared that He came to fulfill, not to destroy, its teachings.[3]

What we call the Lord's Supper was instituted by Jesus at a Jewish ritual meal. "He died with the daily evening prayer of every Jewish home on His lips."[4]

Pope Pius XII was therefore completely right and biblically obedient when he said that "spiritually we are all Semites." Consequently, when I say that for me Jesus Christ is a Jew, the inescapable implication is that I cannot be an authentic and honest Christian apart from this understanding that Jesus was authentically and honestly a Jew. I have a feeling that the story of the tenth Jew, which I recounted earlier, leaves many Christians vaguely uneasy—rather like a Sunday school teacher of my boyhood who felt obliged to mention that, well, of course, Jesus did have Jewish *parents*. But the Sunday school teacher was more than a little embarrassed to acknowledge that Semitic skeleton in the Christian closet. Such uneasiness, embarrassment, and unhistorical selectivity, however, only prove how deep-dyed guilty we are of the blasphemy of anti-Semitism. Anti-Semitism is a sin, one is startled to discover, from the first pages of the New Testament, through the life and literature of the church, right down to the present day. Notice that I said, in deliberately strong language, the "blasphemy

---

[3] Evelyn Underhill, *Worship* (New York: Harper & Brothers, 1937), p. 193.
[4] Ibid., p. 194.

of anti-Semitism." Anti-Semitism is not just a regrettable and culturally conditioned attitude, nor is it even enough to call it a sin. It is blasphemy—not only disrespect for fellow humans but irreverence toward God. Blasphemy is the opposite of honoring the name and nature of God. If, as we believe, Christ is God's presence manifest in a human life (Emmanuel, "God with us"), then disrespect for God's people from whom Christ came is nothing less and nothing other than disrespect—blasphemy—against God.[5]

Jesus is for me teacher and example as well as Jew. He is, as I shall insist later, more than teacher and example, but he is not less. Many years ago, Bishop E. L. Waldorf spoke of the place of Jesus as teacher and example in a way that has become unforgettable for me:

> In the old days we had copy-books given to us, and the "top line" of each page was printed for us as a pattern . . . every stroke properly formed. As long as we kept the "top line" in view we were likely to write a fair copy for ourselves, but by the time we had written three or four lines, we forgot about the "top line" and copied the lines we ourselves had already written. . . . The life of Christ is the "top line," which we ought to imitate, and always

---

[5] "Every form of anti-Semitism is a betrayal of trust in the historical Jesus, on the one hand, and the erection of a Jesus-cult for paganism on the other. Trusting Jesus can only bring us closer to Judaism, not farther from it, for it was in Israel's God that he trusted and to whom he committed those who trust him. If today Jew and Christian will not agree in their stance toward Jesus, it is less because of Jesus than because of the Christian betrayal of him. The tragedy of the original, and repeated, Jewish refusal of Jesus has long since been overshadowed by the Christian betrayal of him as a Jew" (Leander E. Keck, *Future for the Historical Jesus* [Nashville: Abingdon, 1971], p. 191).

keep in view. How often we lose sight of this, and think only of our past experiences, or the lives of professing Christians![6]

To be sure, a danger hides here, just as concentrating one-sidedly on any image of the many-sided Christ is precarious. The danger is that by emphasizing the magnificent teachings of Jesus, we may come to presume that we have lived up to those teachings.

This is a danger in church attendance and effective preaching. (In fact, in some respects, the more effective the preaching, the greater the danger.) Week by week we hear lofty teachings examined, great ideals commended. Unless we are very, very careful, we can come to presume that because we have *heard* about the teachings, we have *done* something about them. *Listening is not learning unless it leads to being.* We may listen to great and stirring sermons about peace yet never lift a finger for peace. We may listen to convinced calls for brotherhood and sisterhood without ever being convinced enough to *be* the brothers or sisters who are being called for.

Nonetheless, Jesus as teacher and example is a permanent and necessary part of who Christ is for us. We are forever in need of keeping our eyes on that perfectly written top line. Christ "grades" the paper of our life and marks it (usually marks it down) according to his own most stringent standards. Some carelessly say that Jesus is "only" an example or teacher. Only? Ah, but that only is *only* the best and the brightest

---

[6]*Evangelism: Heralds of the Good News* (Evanston, Ill.: Garrett Biblical Institute, 1933), p. 11.

example ever managed among the daughters and sons of earth. That only is *only* the loftiest teaching ever shown and shared in our midst.

Furthermore, one aspect of Christ as example is the one we almost always overlook because it is so costly. Peter speaks of it in his first epistle. He says to his little flock: "Christ suffered for you and left you a personal example, so that you might follow in his footsteps." (2:21, Phillips). To follow Jesus as example is not merely to learn some lessons, like sums in school or stories in Sunday school. It is to say with him, and mean it, in Lowell's words, "Christ, thy bleeding feet we track." He only promised us a Gethsemane Garden.

If Christ as Jew is our forefather, Christ as teacher is our elder brother in the faith.

Moreover, for me Christ is not only Jew and teacher, he is savior.

Some of the better theology being written these days comes from the pen of Charles M. Schulz. It appears regularly in the guise of a comic strip entitled "Peanuts." Schulz is responsible for such immortal lines as: "No problem is so big or so complicated that it can't be run away from!" or "The wages of sin is 'Aaaughh!'" In one strip poor Charlie Brown has been forced by his friends to sleep outdoors in a cardboard box without a top. Charlie Brown lies there in misery, looks up toward heaven, and asks, "Why do I have to sleep outside in a cardboard box?" Then, having a second thought, he quickly cries heavenward, "Don't answer that!"

Most of us, I suspect, really know in our innards why

The Question of Identity

we have to be in the box and why we cannot fall asleep. We even surmise that we made the box ourselves, often without intending to. We know, when we are heart honest, that we got ourselves into our moral fix. And—most important—we finally find that we cannot get out of the box and back into the house on our own.

When we discover that, then biblically speaking, we are ready to discover—and accept—Christ as savior.

I do not really understand very much of the rhetoric about Christ's saving us from our sins. Some that I do understand I can't stomach. I don't even fully understand the box I'm stuck in. "Who will deliver me from this?" (Rom. 7:24) cries Paul, for me. "He will deliver us . . . again" (II Cor. 1:10), promises Paul, for us.

Hence when I testify that for me Christ is Savior, my eyes are more upon the stars than upon the box, less upon what Christ saved me *from* than upon what he saves me *for*. The Hebrew word for *salvation* means "to free," "to break the bonds," "to give room." Christ, the book of Ephesians tells us, has taken "captivity captive" (4:8 KJV). *Jesus who is Christ, my savior, has led the greatest prison break in history and has invited me and you and everyone to follow him over the wall.* The important thing is not the cell he broke us out of but the world he sends us into.

It was Irenaeus, in the second century, who spoke of Christ as a prediction. Oh, Christ is also a reminder—a reminder of the dank cell and the dark nights and the black hopelessness. But more—and now—he is a prediction of the freedom and the brightness and the hope that can be yours and mine. His life is an invitation to make that prophecy come true: life made clean and whole, lean and ready, resolute and growing, when finally we decide to follow him out from our miseries into his mercies over the wall and out into the light. "Beloved," I've heard John cry, "it does not yet appear what we shall be, but we know that . . . we shall be like him" (I John 3:2).

Jesus Christ is not only my forefather as Jew and my elder brother as teacher but my forerunner as savior.

I have never found my faith in Jesus Christ easy. I smile in sad amusement at those persons who imagine that faith is easy, whether they be easy skeptics or easy believers. Yet I have never been quite able to forget the vision of Jesus going over the prison wall, nor am I able to withhold my hand as he reaches down to hoist me up to freedom with him. Jesus Christ is at once the profoundest problem and the severest challenge of my life. Indeed he *is* my life.

I am glad to be able to say in unison with Peter, "You are the Christ," and I am grateful that we are no longer commanded to keep that gladness and that grace to ourselves.

Through Jesus Christ, "our teacher, example, and Redeemer, the savior of the world. Amen."

VI
The Question of Compassion
"Who Is My Neighbor?"
Luke 10:29

Did you ever break a thermometer and then try to pick up the escaping pellets of mercury between your thumb and forefinger? The more you try, the more the little silver balls separate into tinier pieces and roll away.

The word *neighbor* is similarly hard to get hold of. In our time, the notion of neighbor is fractured, mobile, and elusive.

The earth, which once was a pumpkin, is now a pea. Apartment walls are so thin that one man can say, "I'll have some ketchup," and a second later, another man in the next apartment finds himself eating a bleeding egg. National walls are made of glass—and not bulletproof glass either. The American secretary of state coughs in the middle of the night, and the Russian premier stirs in his sleep. A black man is jailed in Mississippi, and a white man in Missouri reaches for his checkbook to help provide bail. A man or woman can have breakfast with his or her family in the Midwest, lunch with a publisher in New York, yet be home in time to watch the evening news on television.

The word *neighbor*, my dictionary tells me, once meant "nigh dweller," or "one who lives near." In these ancient terms, the whole modern world is a neighborhood. Everybody lives near everybody. In these modern terms, the young lawyer's ancient question "Who is my neighbor?" has to be retranslated: "Who isn't my neighbor?"

But that retranslation does not really answer either question. It only gives it greater urgency if we do not know what is meant by *neighbor* in the first place. Today, to make it all the tougher, we find that those we once called "foreigners have become neighbors and the neighbors have become foreigners."[1]

No wonder, then, that moderns (crowded and jarred, scared and scarred by more neighbors than they know what to do with) perk up their ears at this old-new question, Who *is* my neighbor?

If we have read our New Testament, we already met the young man questioning Jesus. Matthew, the Arthur Miller of the New Testament writers, introduced this chap, the Rich Young Ruler, into the scenario of his Gospel (19:16-22). In both Matthew and Luke the young

[1] Charles W. Forman, *A Faith for the Nations* (Philadelphia: Westminster Press, 1957), p. 10.

The Question of Compassion

man begins with substantially the same question, "What shall I do to inherit eternal life?" (Luke 10:25; Matt. 19:16). Both times Jesus talks with him about the law of love for God and neighbor.

Even if someone had not overheard the conversation and recorded the Master's approving response, "You have answered right" (Luke 10:28), we could be sure that Jesus would take no exception to the fellow's answer. How could he? Jesus had himself given this answer on at least two occasions. He knew that these two commandments "Love God—love neighbor" were yokefellows. The men are thus agreed: If one has not found the neighbor, one has not found God. Here out of the entire 613 Jewish laws, the young rabbi and the young lawyer found two to agree upon as most important. This at least made the situation simpler. So what was wrong? Why did Jesus turn away the lawyer's question, as a fencer parries a thrust?

What was wrong was that, as Luke tells us, the questioner wanted "to justify himself" (10:29). He had already asked one question. He had got only another question in return ("What is written in the law? How do you read?"). "But it isn't that easy," thought the lawyer, "I cannot let him off at that. I will try again." So he did, in an attempt to vindicate his original question and to show that the whole business was not as simple as Jesus' answer seemed to imply. "Love thy neighbor as thyself? Yes, true enough. But tell me now, what do you mean by 'neighbor'?" Since it was a lawyer speaking, I suspect Luke had to edit his language for lay people. In the unrevised standard version it probably listened something like this: "Whereas Party

Are You the Christ?

of the First Part, to wit, a lawyer from Jerusalem, and Party of the Second Part, to wit, a rabbi from Nazareth, are in substantial agreement upon the primacy of neighbor-love, now therefore, be it resolved that Party of the Second Part provide the aforementioned with his operational definition of neighbor."

Instead of answering the lawyer directly, Jesus told him a story! Told *him*—a summa cum laude graduate of the College of Law, University of Jerusalem—a story: a simple, silly little thing about a road on which there were too few cops and too many robbers and a foreigner who was not even important enough for anyone to remember his name.

Talk about being insulted! Do you show second-grade flash cards to Einstein? Do you read nursery rhymes to T. S. Eliot? Do you ask a graduate engineer if he can fix your erector set? Come now—answer my question!

But what Jesus was saying to the youth is that you cannot get at the problem this way, any more than you can irrigate the desert with a sprinkling can. The question is not about your duty but about your attitude. Nevertheless, it was clever of him to try, was it not? If we can cast doubt upon who the neighbor is, we may be able to escape any obligation to him.

Most of us know, without much fuss, how we are supposed to act toward neighbors. But we play a fearful game of intellectual dodgeball with the question of who the neighbor is. The Protestant asks, "Is a Catholic my neighbor—even a bigoted one?" The Gentile asks, "Is a Jew my neighbor—even an obnoxious one?" The white man asks, "Is a black my neighbor—even a pushy one?" The distinguished professor asks, "Is a mere undergraduate my neighbor—even an agnostic one?" We know we are not really inquiring or asking. We are escaping—or trying to.

II

The story Jesus told, then, was essentially a flanking maneuver designed to cut off escape.

It is a familiar story, though strangely we cannot tell it often enough—or well enough. The road that the man took down from Jerusalem to Jericho was called in those days the bloody way. Its limestone caves and sharp turns were as dangerous as an urban alley at midnight. The prudent person wanting to travel the seventeen miles between the two cities took a traveling companion along that steep road that drops some thirteen hundred feet enroute. One man, though, forgot, and was mugged for his carelessness. The priest and the Levite, as they passed him by, no doubt thanked God that they had been spared such a fate.

Here is where Jesus "gets personal," as we put it. For the hero of his little tale was a Samaritan. A Samaritan!—a person whose word no Jew believed and whose testimony no Jewish court accepted. Indeed, not only was the hero a non-Jew, but he was a layman. Nevertheless, even though he had not studied in the best theological seminaries and probably could not tell the Passover from a picnic, he "was moved with compassion" (Luke 10:33b, literal translation). *Moved.* In other words, he did something about it. He did not just think about it, he was motivated by it. He administered first aid, put the injured man on his beast, walked beside him to an inn, spent the equivalent of two days' wages to pay for his keep, and told the innkeeper there was more where that came from.

The priest and the Levite in this story are not "they." Rather they are we. Actually, in a way, they were loving their neighbor as themselves. The trouble was that they thought of themselves as priests and Levites. Since the man in the ditch was neither, they could not have cared less for him. Sound familiar? Sure we love our neighbors as ourselves—white, Gentile, Protestant, middle-class, educated, American neighbors. Those people in Jesus' story really get around. Today they are called the Reverend John Wesley Priest or Mr. Uncle Sam Levite. They wear wide ties, mod boots, and drive from Jerusalem to Jericho, from home to church, from home to lab, or from home state to Congress. But it is just an old movie with new actors and updated dialogue.

And the Samaritan? He has changed his garb and talks with a little different accent, but he is still around. How often have we Christians been shamed by the genuine idealism and practical piety of those who cannot or will not call themselves Christians? I am reminded of a newspaper editor in an Indiana city. He is a kind of Harry Golden of the Midwest. The city in which his paper is published had been debating for years whether to engage in a much-needed slum-clearance project. Some time back a shack in the shabby heart of that slum burned down, and the lives of two little children were snuffed out. The clergy, who

The Question of Compassion

presumably had heard something about the Master's love for little children, were sinfully silent. The politicians engaged in debate with renewed fervor, throwing around phrases like "individual rights" and "federal control" as if they were tossing a verbal salad for their constituents' consumption. But who got mad *for God's sake?* The Samaritan editor did. Old pagan Paul took another chomp on his ever-present cigar and wrote a city-blistering, excuse-exploding editorial that must have made glad the heart of God.

My guess is that he had visited the scene of the civic crime, gone out to the charred ashes, and run his shoe through the blackened remains until perhaps it came up hard against a tin cup or a toy pistol, until he saw the whole horrible thing through that blessed anger we call righteous indignation. That, at least, is what happened to the original Samaritan. When he *saw* him, he was moved with compassion. That is what it takes, really, seeing through to the other side of the statistics until the handicapped child on the poster becomes your child or your little brother. The priest and the Levite saw only themselves—and so walked heedlessly on. The Samaritan saw a face—that is, a neighbor—and so knelt helpfully down.

III

The question Jesus really answered was not the dutiful, Who is my neighbor? but, Whose neighbor am I? He was saying that our attitude toward others should

Are You the Christ?

"not depend upon who they are but upon who we are."[2]

I said at the outset of this chapter that the young lawyer's question has to be retranslated for our time: Who isn't my neighbor? However, if this problem is ever to come home for us, it must be upon the shrinking territory of our time, in which "crisis has become routine, catastrophe moves on ball bearings, death is efficiently administered and unsentimentally cleaned up, terror is commonplace and melodrama humdrum."[3]

In the back of my brain is one lobe that, I am convinced, was not baptized with all the rest. At any rate, it chuckled with the devil's glee at the following misprint in the press. The reference is to a speaker coming to town who, it was said, was a delegate to the Assembly of the *Worldly* Council of Churches. But after I got through enjoying the linotypist's bad luck and the proofreader's even worse eyesight, I thought to myself: "The *worldly* council of churches? Of course. It had better be. That's what the Good Samaritan story is all about—worldliness—in the roadside, ditch-descending sense."[4] One of the old Germans, the elder Christoph Blumhardt used to say, "Every Christian needs two conversions, first to Christ and then to the world."

The heresy Jesus is trying to combat with this story of

[2] James K. Matthews, *To the End of the Earth* (Nashville: Methodist Student Movement, 1959), p. 59.
[3] Frederic Morton, "The Sweetness of Death," *Saturday Review*, 22 May 1954, p. 14.
[4] I have the uneasy feeling that I have borrowed this illustration from someone else. If so, I cannot locate the source in either my memory or my notes.

The Question of Compassion

the Good Samaritan is one of the oldest and most persistent heresies of all; namely, that the church, like the priest and the Levite, is to go on about its religious business and leave the world to its own devices. It was illustrated again, in bureaucratic form, when the Internal Revenue Service announced that it had revoked the tax-exempt status of the Fellowship of Reconciliation (FOR). (More recently other church-related enterprises have been threatened with the same action.) The Fellowship of Reconciliation is one of our most effective peace organizations. Yet consider the utterly fantastic reasons the Internal Revenue gave for this revocation. Those eminent theologians in Washington asserted that (1) the pursuit of peace is a political, not a religious, activity (Jesus would have been interested in that judgment) and (2) FOR is an action organization, while only "education," as distinct from "action," groups are eligible for exemption. On those grounds the church should be ashamed of its exemption.[5] If a dazed churchman may be permitted a question at this point, he should like to ask, Are the churches of America going to be *doers* of the word and not *hearers* only? For a religion that is not worldly in this sense cannot be Christian in any sense.

That unbaptized section of my brain got another jolt some time ago. Glancing through the want ads of a local paper, I came upon this advertisement, which

---

[5] The question of tax exemption for churches and church-related institutions is legitimately debatable and may well deserve review. That is not the issue here. Rather, what I am referring to is the absurd and covertly theological assumptions informing this decision.

read in part: "For rent—sleeping rooms for Christians." I fell to thinking: How do Christians sleep differently from others? Do we sleep more soundly because we trust God? Do we sleep less because there is so much that desperately needs doing yet so little time, perhaps, in which to do it?

There is, at any rate, much in our world to keep us from occupying those sleeping rooms: the hot threat of war and the cold war of threats; the snail's pace of racial justice that at the present rate will have all schools integrated in only 17,746 years; the Northern version of racial bigotry that exists on your block or in the deed to your house or in the membership requirements of your favorite organization; understaffed and overcrowded mental hospitals; a world in which nearly a thousand babies have been born since you began to read this chapter; a world in which the average Chinese weighs eighteen pounds less than the average European and in which the East Indian farmer gains one-fifth the cotton per acre harvested by his American counterpart; a church in which Christians sing, "Give of your sons to bear the message glorious" but whose members then subtly influence their own sons and daughters to choose some field more "practical" than the ministry.

Surely here, somewhere, is something to keep you awake—some place where you are needed and can be used, some haunting roadside cry from a world that has been beaten and left half dead, some wounds that need your oil and wine, some neighbor's face from whom you dare not avert your eyes or withhold your hand or walk away. For the real question is not, Who is my neighbor? but, Whose neighbor am I?

This is, of course, no proper place to end this chapter. But no matter. Whose *neighbor* are *you*? You answer the question—in your own time and in your own way.

VII
The Easter Verb

Gerard Manley Hopkins demonstrated in a single line that he was a daring poet. In "The Wreck of the *Deutschland*" he wrote: "Let him easter in us, be a dayspring to the dimness of us." This great British Jesuit, who was almost totally overlooked in his lifetime, was not only a richly associative poet, but also, in this line, an insightful theologian. Who of us would have thought to make *easter* a verb?

What I want to suggest in this concluding chapter is that, in a sense, Hopkins borrowed that idea (if not that line), as T. S. Eliot says somewhere all good poets do. Specifically, he borrowed it from the New Testament.

The Easter Verb

I

Easter is usually referred to and celebrated as a noun: an event, an occurrence, a thing or a series of things that took place in that small bracket of time between Friday's cruciform blackness and Sunday's clarifying light. Too many discussions of Easter (if I am any judge) leave the impression that Easter *was* something that *happened once.*

But to say that Easter happened only once is to come perilously close to suggesting that it happened "once upon a time," which is the parlance we sometimes employ to express our suspicion that something did not in fact occur at all. It is Jack-in-the-Beanstalk language or, at best, Joan-of-Arc- and-her-mysterious-voices language: "Once upon a time."

Part of the reason behind the once-upon-a-time attitude is that the church has focused upon the Gospel Easter stories in the wrong way. We have allowed these stories to become merely proper nouns—too proper, in fact—to the extent that they exclude the verb they point to, namely, *Jesus' having eastered in them.* But this way lies confusion, contradiction, and often disbelief.

The New Testament narratives are a welter of enigmas in which space and time, matter and spirit, have been shaken up in a bag and then dumped out before our eyes in glorious disarray. Time gets all mixed up: the thief on the cross, it is said, will be in paradise three days before Christ's own resurrection. Matter gets all mixed up: Thomas is invited to do what Mary Magdalene is forbidden, namely, to touch the risen body. Spirit gets all mixed up: Christ walks through a closed door in the Upper Room, which sounds as if John is suggesting a spiritual, nonmaterial presence; Christ sits down to supper and breaks bread, which sounds as if Luke is describing a physical presence. The Easter Symphony thunders with dissonance. For our part, it is far better to admit that it clashes harsh upon the ear than to transpose it into an incidental ditty with a forced harmony.

Let us switch the metaphor. These Gospel narratives are a great scriptural seismograph, recording the tremors caused at the place where God once thundered. But you cannot hear thunder by analyzing a seismograph. To credit as fact a report that it thundered last week or two thousand years ago is not to feel the thunder's terror and power now. To paraphrase Hopkins' prayerful line, we must "let him thunder in us." So John Donne said: "I have a grave of sin. . . . Where Lazarus had been four days, I have been for fifty years. Why dost Thou not call me, as Thou didst him? I need Thy thunder, O my God; Thy music will not serve me."[1]

II

The Easter stories are a kind of theological applause meter, recording the responses of that "first morning" audience.[2] But the divine play continues to run. Its

---

[1] Quoted by Paul Scherer in *The Word God Sent* (New York: Harper & Row, 1965), p. 140.
[2] I owe this metaphor, and the previous one about the seismograph, to the late Carl Michalson.

The Easter Verb

opening performance was Easter. Its continuing effect is eastering.

At the risk of turning this chapter into an essay on English grammar, I want to say something about the function of verbs. My friends in English departments remind me that verbs are of two kinds, transitive and intransitive. "A transitive verb is one that acts as a transmission belt, conveying action or influence from a subject to an object."[3] For instance, in the sentence "Kareem Abdul-Jabar dunks the ball . . ." or "Little Orphan Annie wears contact lenses," *dunks and wears* are transitive verbs. An intransitive verb, on the other hand, is self-contained. It stops with itself. The sentences "The governor has spoken" or "Cabinet officers will economize" contain intransitive verbs.

Now back to our title, "The Easter Verb." The same transitive-intransitive distinction is important. We may say transitively, "In A.D. 29, God eastered." It is God—the Eternal Subject—I am stressing. "In A.D. 29, God *eastered*." For instance, some scholars believe that the original form of the Lord's Prayer did not include the ascription of praise with which it now closes. Certainly, it did not. It was a Resurrection community that had to add to our Lord's words, "for thine is the kingdom and the power and the glory forever and ever. Amen." I say *had* to add because that power had overpowered them; its glory had appeared to them. For another instance, it is significant to note that the Protestant Episcopal Church prescribes for reading on

---

[3] Theodore M. Bernstein, *The Careful Writer* (New York: Atheneum, 1965), p. 254.

Are You the Christ?

Easter the moving Old Testament story about God mercifully passing over the children of Israel and miraculously delivering his beleaguered people from the hands of their enemies, a motif that one of the Easter hymns picks up and extends as: "God hath brought his people forth."

When God eastered, the big question was settled. The big question was whether God is in fact God—whether God rules the Pilates and the Herods; the mobs and the soldiers; the Judas Iscariots and the Simon Peters; the nails, the swords, the thorns, and the grave—or whether God is rather ruled by them, defeated by them, which would mean, of course, that God is not God. That ultimate question was settled, once and for all, by the eastering God. When we make easter a verb, we are dealing first of all with a great fact about God.

All of this, so well known to the faith and to the faithful, is gloriously true. Indeed if it were not known and true, I would not have written (and you would not be reading) this book. If it were not known and true, the faith we gladly name as our own would have died in some dusty Latin footnote before the end of the first century A.D., though we would not have dated it so, save for what God decisively did in Christ.

The first Christians felt this in their bones. Consequently, they early came to call Jesus Emmanuel. *Emmanuel* was originally a common noun, but it quickly became a proper name: Emmanuel, meaning "God with us." But Jesus' status and standing as an object of faith (as a noun) springs out of a deeper rootage as a verb: Emmanuel, the *coming-to-us-God*.

Theirs was not a God of being but of doing, not one who merely exists but one who mightily comes.

Thus the point I want to make in this chapter concerns the strength of *easter* as a transitive verb, the transmitting of something to us, something that has come to us in no other way. Having acknowledged and rehearsed what God has done, I am calling you to recognize and celebrate what God has done *in us*— eastered in us. Resurrection is not only something to be remembered and contemplated; it is a process to be renewed and continued. Paul calls Christ "the first to be harvested" (I Cor. 15:20, author's translation), which clearly implies that he is not the last. Marcus Barth, the son of the late great Swiss theologian Karl Barth, has asserted that Christ's "resurrection is a miracle which affects our being as radically and miraculously as it affected him who was buried in the garden."[4]

III

Hopkins has another poem, the title of which nicely addresses and expresses our theme. It is called "What I Do Is Me," and it reads: "As kingfishers catch fire, dragonflies draw flame"—as stones ring when tumbled into wells, as a bell finds, swinging, a clapper tongue "to fling out broad its name." So, sings the poet,

> Myself it speaks and spells,
> Crying *What I do is me: for that I came.*

[4] Quoted in Paul S. Minear, *Images of the Church in the New Testament* (Philadelphia: Westminster Press, 1960), p. 200.

Then, the poet adds, beginning to make verbs of events and values,

> The just man justices; . . .
> Acts in God's eyes what in God's eye he is.

The just man, he is saying, makes justice a verb. He embodies justice—acts it out. He is what he does. What he does shapes what he is and is becoming.

We have a parable of this in the unusual work of John Rosen, a psychiatrist:

> Conventional psychotherapy, as you know, is practiced with people sometimes paradoxically called "normal neurotics," i.e., people whose disturbances are not so deep or overwhelming that they have lost the power of speech. Conventional psychotherapy depends on the exchange of words. But patients with deep psychoses often slip into catatonia, through long stretches of which they live in apparently impenetrable silence. How can the psychiatrist reach them? How can he rouse them even to the level where conventional psychotherapy can begin?
>
> For the period during which he is going to work with a group of these most deeply disturbed patients, Dr. Rosen moves in on their ward, placing his bed right alongside theirs. On the initial morning having addressed a patient with "Good morning," and having received no response ("Surely he is aware," whisper the knowing nurses, "that that man hasn't spoken in ten years!"), Rosen suddenly strips off his coat, tie, and shirt . . . He then begins the most intimate kind of mothering and loving. He loves and embraces the patient again and again, wordlessly, employing only this primitive language of gesture. He follows the same procedure a second, third, fourth day,

The Easter Verb

sometimes for weeks, conveying to the patient in the most fundamental, altogether preverbal language man possesses, the language of gesture, that he *is* loved. And slowly, after varying periods of time, many patients are loved back into speech. Their first words are often a halting, "Thank you."[5]

Thus we sometimes speak of "doctoring," because the physician has made an active verb of his art.

It must have been some such insight that prompted Martin Luther King, Jr., to say to a friend, "We are not truly alive *until our names are verbs,* instead of nouns."[6] In Dr. King's dramatic case, it is not difficult to sense what that means. This nation can be said, justifiably, to have been "kinged" toward justice. That is because this man who did it to us and in us was unwilling to be merely the titular head of a movement. Instead, he insisted upon pouring out his love, acting out his anguish, staking out claims in the conscience of his countrymen, and finally giving up his life for them. His name became and continues to be a verb in our midst.

Perhaps you need to ask yourself what it would mean if your name became a verb, in whatever small but specific way God calls you along.

And—no "perhaps" about it—the reason the Bible cries of its Lord, "Therefore God has highly exalted him and bestowed on him the name which is above every name" (Phil. 2:9), is that his name became a verb, a

---

[5] Quoted in John D. Maguire, *The Dance of the Pilgrim* (New York: Association Press, 1967), pp. 96-97.
[6] Quoted in Kent Hull, "The Open Hand," *Christian Century.*

Are You the Christ?

healing, a saying, a doing, and a living that humankind cannot permanently escape or safely ignore.

Paul seems to point to this verbing of our destiny when he testifies to the Galatians, "I have been crucified with Christ; it is no longer I who live, but Christ who lives in me" (2:20a). Paul's life thereafter, gifted and uplifted by the Christ alive in him, is a torrent of outgoing verbs—preaching and loving, trusting and living. Christ lives in me, thunders in me, easters in me.

IV

And does Christ live in us?—in you and me?

He easters your sorrows, your "pain too big for tears,"[7] your tears too deep for words, your thirsty loneliness seemingly too stark for slaking. Yet the book not accidentally called "The New Testament of our Lord and Savior Jesus Christ" draws near its close with the mighty affirmation: "He will wipe away every tear from their eyes, and death shall be no more, neither shall there be mourning nor crying nor pain any more" (Rev. 21:4a). He easters our sorrows.

He also easters our hopes. It is no accident that the Bible uses the word *hope* 158 times, the word *hopeless* only twice: "Blessed be the God and Father of our Lord Jesus Christ! By his great mercy we have been born anew to a living hope through the resurrection of Jesus Christ" (I Peter 1:3).

Thales, that so-called wise man of ancient Greece,

[7] Ralph Ellison, *The Invisible Man* (New York: Random House, 1951), p. 100.

may be excused for his shallow dictum "Hope is the poor man's bread." But, in point of Christian fact, hope is the devout person's crown. It has eastered its way into our hearts and refuses to budge from its throne.

Christ also easters our humanity. As a result we need no longer be an insoluble problem to ourselves. In Jesus Christ, what it means to be a human is defined, declared, and demonstrated. In him we learn at last that, although we may be brought to nothing, we cannot be reduced to nothing. He has eastered in us—in us, by God. And so, "When anyone is united to Christ, there is a new act of creation" (II Cor. 5:17 NEB, alternate reading).

Recall now Hopkins' other phrase, in which he prays that Christ will "be a dayspring to the dimness in us." The poet prayed that way because, as a Christian, he was repeating an announcement that preceded the birth of Christ: "Through the tender mercy of God; whereby the dayspring from on high hath visited us" (Luke 1:78 KJV). *Dayspring*, remember, is biblical shorthand for the beginning of a new era. That is our faith. Christ is eastering in us. He is the dayspring to the dimness in us. Therefore, "Thanks be to God, who gives us the victory, through our Lord Jesus Christ" (I Cor. 15:57).

Index of Scripture

Old Testament

Exodus
  10:21 56
Numbers
  11:16 39
II Chronicles
  1:10 36
II Kings
  13:23 23
Proverbs
  8:35 36
Isaiah
  40:31a 54
  61:1 31
  66:9a, 13, 14 56
Daniel
  7:13 62

New Testament

Matthew
  5:44 46
  6:10c 54
  6:26 21
  6:34 46
  7:29 44
  8:23-27 15-25
  8:24 16
  8:25 19
  8:26 19
  8:27 .... 16-17, 18, 19, 21, 22, 24
  10:16 55
  10:22a 55
  10:39 47
  12:3 45
  16:16 64
  18:12 45
  19:16 75
  19:16-22 74
  26:18 47
Mark
  1:44 39
  4:38b 19
  6:1-6a 26-36
  6:2 28
  6:2b-3a 27-28
  6:3 29
  6:4a 32
  6:4 33
  11:17 40
  14:61 62
  14:61b-62 63

Mark (continued)
14:69 62

Luke
1:78 93
4:18 31
4:21 31
4:22a 27
4:28 27
8:24b, 25b 21
10:3 55
10:25 75
10:28 75
10:29 73-83
10:33-34 23
10:33b 77
12:57 45
20:1-8 37-49
20:1 38
20:2 38
22:66-71 61-72
22:67a 62
22:69 62
22:71 63

John
14:9a 62
14:27 22
15:11 58-59
15:14 46
16:16-24 50-60
16:16 51
16:17 52
16:17, 18 .... 51, 54
16:19 53
16:21-22 52

16:23-24 57
16:24 58
16:32 21
17:13 58

Romans
7:24 71
8:18 59
8:28, 31, 35, 37-39 60

I Corinthians
13:12 62
15:20 89
15:57 93

II Corinthians
1:10 71
5:17 93

Galatians
2:20a 92

Ephesians
4:8 71

Philippians
2:5 57
2:7-8 46
2:9 91

Hebrews
12:1 65

Titus
3:9 29

James
3:17 35

I Peter
2:21 70
5:9 55

I John
3:2 72